Soccer Analytics

Chest Dugger

Contents

ABOUT THE AUTHOR 3

DISCLAIMER 4

Introduction 5

How Analytics Are Used In Soccer 6

Team Formation Analytics 14

Attacking Set Play Analytics 24

Defensive Set Play Analytics 35

Player Performance Analytics 41

Player Injury Analytics 50

Player Combination Analytics 55

Case Studies 59

Conclusion 71

ABOUT THE AUTHOR

Chest Dugger is a soccer fan, former professional and coach, looking to share his knowledge. Enjoy this book and several others that he has written.

DISCLAIMER

Copyright © 2018

All Rights Reserved

No part of this eBook can be transmitted or reproduced in any form including print, electronic, photocopying, scanning, mechanical, or recording without prior written permission from the author.

While the author has taken the utmost effort to ensure the accuracy of the written content, all readers are advised to follow information mentioned herein at their own risk. The author cannot be held responsible for any personal or commercial damage caused by information. All readers are encouraged to seek professional advice when needed.

Introduction

Many thanks for purchasing this book. Analytics are playing an increasing role in the world of soccer. The days of gut instinct representing the main tactic in a game are passing, and a more calculated approach is being applied to coaching and playing.

This has the advantage of providing a secure base on which coaches and players can apply their bits of skill, their touches of magic that can turn a game. This book will explain what soccer analytics are, and how they work in a game.

It will analyse different parts of play during a game and provide ideas and details around how analytics can improve a team during various passages of play. It will show that it is possible to carry out analytics without recourse to expensive software and the kind of backroom team that is only possible in the higher levels of the professional game.

We hope that you find it interesting, and informative. And that it makes your team, your coaching or your own play more effective.

How Analytics Are Used In Soccer

The former England manager, Sam Allardyce, was the ground breaker when it came to using analytics in English soccer. His use of the programme 'Prozone' when manager of Bolton Wanderers in the early part of the century led the way for the extensive use we have today.

Poor Sam, as fans will know, was the England manager England didn't really have. Following his one game in charge, he was caught in a press sting, when he was recorded having a conversation with a journalist acting as a fake agent. The recordings exposed the most tenuous of links to under hand payments during which Sam promised nothing, said nothing wrong and offered nothing untoward.

But the English FA is the English FA, stuck in the past and notoriously duplicitous – Sam had to go. Indeed, if the FA had its way, England would probably be playing the game with a leather ball and long shorts using a tape as the bar on the goal.

A Bit Of History

But Big Sam, as he is known across the Atlantic (now doing an amazing job taking an under performing team, Everton, up the Premier

League where they belong), was not the originator of analytics. For that we can probably head back to the 1950s and Charles Reep. He had been a Wing Commander in the air force and, on leaving that, became a consultant for a number of soccer teams. In the days pre-computer, he would track matches, recording various details of passing moves, dribbles, tackles, combinations that led goal attempts and so forth.

His conclusion was that most goals came after a set of three passes or fewer and were often the result of a counterattack. That last point is as true today as it was over sixty years ago. If we look at the best and most successful teams in the world's leading leagues we will see that one of the tactics they use is the ability to turn defence quickly into attack. These teams have the ability to be effective in the transition parts of the game and turn a quick break into a goal creating opportunity.

However, there is more to these teams than this. Getting the ball forward quickly is not effective in terms of the overall result unless defence is strong, because a team playing 'on the break' will spend long periods without the ball. Charles Hughes was technical director of the English FA for a period which encompassed 'the golden generation' of English footballers. But the team, which was filled with attacking talent, creative midfielders and dogged defenders, achieved nothing beyond the odd World Cup quarter final. Many today lay the problem at Hughes' door, because he advocated an approach that relied on getting the ball forward quickly. His evidence was analytics from a single World Cup, France 98, where he saw that a majority of goals came from few passes and getting the ball forward quickly.

The result was a team that tried to get the ball forward fast, through a long, direct ball. This often meant missing out the talented midfield. Consequently, possession was lost too easily, and England were defeated by teams able to keep the ball and create spaces for goal attempts.

Hughes should be praised for being prepared to use data to underpin his technical theories, but that data was not complete, and this is a good example of using analytics out of context of the game as a whole.

Clearly, these days the theory that more passes equal increased chances of losing the ball is no longer as relevant. Playing surfaces are better, improved training – not least because of the growth of analytics – means that players are technically more adept and therefore pass and control the ball better.

So, having taken a brief glance at the history of soccer analytics, let us now move on to see how they are employed in the modern game.

What, Exactly, Are Analytics?

Firstly, we need to define what exactly is meant by the term, analytics. When applied in a sporting context, including soccer, we are talking about the processes through which a player's or players' impact on a game can be determined taking into account a variety of data. This data relates to training, team match play and individual performances. The idea is to use that data to maximize the performance of a time, often through raising the quality and effectiveness of performance of individual players.

It can also be applied to opposing teams and players, to work out their strengths and identify weaknesses that could be exploited.

Soccer analytics can be used in many ways. It can allow us to:

- Work out the likely outcome of a game
- Predict the performances of teams
- Predict the performances of individual players
- Build strategies to maximize the chances of winning a match or tournament.

What Can Be Analyzed?

We can broadly divide the scope of analytics in three areas. These are:

Game Modeling

Here, analytics will have identified a number of tactical moves that can be applied to a game situation to turn the outcome in our team's favor. It can be as significant a change as the 'Plan B' so beloved of soccer commentators. In this situation there is a complete alteration of tactics to deal with a problematic situation – for example, a speedy winger is causing all kinds of difficulties for our full back. Our analytics carried out in training will have considered tactical changes for dealing with this situation. It might include switching from a 4-4-2 line up to a 5-3-2 formation to allow an extra defender to support the full back. It may involve a substitution to allow a more defensive player on the pitch.

However, while it provides useful tactical information for a coach to consider during the game, the analytics will have identified the set up a team plans to use. For example, an opponent that likes to utilize a tall set of players from set pieces might lead a coach to set up his own team in a way that restricts the number of corners and attacking free kicks conceded.

Game modeling analytics are also useful for post-match consideration. The analysis of the game post-match can identify key points for a team to build on. For example, a simple phone camera could be used to film every attacking corner. From there, the footage can be analyzed to assess the effectiveness of the corners, and to identify why they are working, or why they fall apart.

Player Ratings

We will look at this factor in more details a little later. However, in this section we analyze the performance, skills and attributes of individual players. This happens both in the match situation and in training. Many players produce their best during the competitiveness of the game; equally, some feel more able to express themselves on the training pitch and can underperform when it comes to a competitive game.

Because the analytics are based on data, the analysis for player ratings are divided into many specific areas. Such areas could be acceleration, speed over 20 metres, quality of first touch, ability to pass with either foot, ability to control swerve, aerial competence under pressure, aerial ability with time and so forth. What emerges is a detailed build up of the strengths and weaknesses of a player. This information can then be used both in team planning and also to help to improve a player by addressing those weaknesses. It is simply applying a scientific approach to what used to be a gut instinct.

'He's no good in the air,' might have been an old-time judgement, based on seeing the player mis-time some clearances. But proper analysis might help a coach to see that the player is very effective at stopping his opponent from winning headed balls. Thus, the defender would work on the quality of his heading when not under direct pressure, while the coach would keep him in the side because he sees that the defender does his job well when up against a forward.

Performance Analytics

Here, the tool helps players and coaches to analyze their performance during matches. It is based on hard data, rather than impressions. For example, the number of touches, the number of successful short passes, successful long passes; the accuracy of shots on goal with the left foot, right foot, under pressure and so forth.

That data both helps a coach and his team to develop tactics to utilize their strengths and also will tell individual players the areas on which they need to work.

In this chapter we have considered what soccer analytics actually are, examined their historical context and explored some of the ways the data can be used by players and coaches. We have also considered some of the forms that the analytics can take. Now we will look at the individual elements of soccer that can be enhanced but the use of analytics, beginning with team formation.

Team Formation Analytics

The range of team formations is wide, and their employment is often a cause of huge discussion. At the end of the day, there are ten players (excluding the goalkeeper, although this player will contribute much to the general team play in the modern game) and they can be utilized in only so many ways.

Primarily, teams tend to adopt one of the following – for beginners to soccer, the numbers start with the defence, move on to midfield and end with attack.

Four – Four – Two: considered old fashioned these days, it is quite a defensive arrangement with the defence and midfield as two secure units. By having four defenders, the opportunities for these players to move forward is limited in open play, since to do so leave the defence short.

Five – Three – Two: very much in vogue, and more attacking than the numbers suggest. The five defenders mean that two full backs can bomb forward to support midfield and attack, leaving enough defenders to cope if the attack breaks down. The formation, with eight or nine players behind the ball also means that breaking up attacks is easier, and then the team can break with speed during the transition of possession. It is a system often played by teams who are effective on the break.

Five – One – Three – One or *Four – Two – Three – One*: Very attacking. The three advanced midfielders support the attack, and the single (or double) midfielder sits, protecting a back three and allowing the wide defenders to get forward.

Four – Five – One: This formation will suit a team with two good wingers who can both get forward and provide midfield cover.

Four – Three – Three: Very attacking, but rarely used these days. The system sees two wingers and a centre-forward. However, it does not allow for a natural Number 10, widely seen as the most creative player in modern formations. Also, having just three midfielders means that teams can be over run in this department, meaning that getting the ball to the attackers happens less often than would be wanted.

From these standard formations, coaches can tinker to try to gain an advantage over the opposition, perhaps keeping a speedy winger at bay, or denying attacking possession to an outstanding passer of the ball.

But the questions remain as to which formation to choose, and how much that should be tinkered about? This is where soccer analytics can come into play.

How To Use Analytics To Decide On The Best Formation

The starting point for any match must be our own team. We can use the analytics we have carried out to identify the strengths and weaknesses of our players. Then, we can build our formation around that.

Let us spend a short time looking at the characteristics we would look for from the various positions on the park. We will exclude the goalkeeper from this analysis. In the paragraphs below, the elements of play that can be assessed using analytics are in bold.

Full Backs

The modern game requires a full back to have excellent **stamina**. We need the player to be a wide attacking outlet, unless we are going to play with out and out wingers. The full back needs to an effective **crosser** of the ball. He or she needs excellent **pace** to out flank defenders and midfielders and the ability to **cross early**, before the opposing defence can get into position. Finally, the ability to **dribble** or **run with the ball** at pace are also crucial to get speed into counter attacks.

Those are some of the attacking qualities needed from this player. Defensively, the position requires **bravery** along with the **determination** to win the one on one contests that will take place with their opposing wide midfielder or winger. The full back needs to be a competent **header** of the ball, or the opposition will seek to isolate them on the far post and send in high, swinging crosses. The player needs to be a good **tackler**.

Central Defenders

Again, it is fair to say that this is a different position in the modern game than it used to be. The old idea of a big, aggressive stopper has been refined. Now the player needs to be more skilled on the ball.

Defensively, a central defender needs excellent **positional sense**, and good **communication**, as this position is usually the one from where the defence is organized. Just as the full back, good **tackling**, remains a good attribute to have. Strong all-round **heading** ability is also necessary.

It is an advantage to have a centre half who possesses some or all of the following attributes, although because the player has one or two colleagues, they are less essential if other team mates do have them. **Comfort on the ball, good passing** and **speed** are all beneficial.

Central Defensive Midfielders

Some might say this is the least glamourous position on the pitch, but whether or not that is true, it is certainly one of the most important. A good central defensive midfielder can allow more creative players to feel confident in their play. It can make defenders feel comfortable about moving forward.

There are two or three essentials in the role. Good **stamina** is a must, as the player will be covering and tackling regularly, plus always making themselves available for the pass. Good **discipline** is a must. It is probably the position in professional football that receives most yellow cards, because it is the key **tackling** position on the park. The ability to **read** the game is also crucial.

Still important, but not absolutely vital, a good **short passing** ability is very useful, and it is no harm to be able to put in **floated** or **weighted** passes. The CDM often arrives late into attacks, perhaps picking up the ball as it is cleared, and therefore the ability to **shoot from distance** is an important weapon in a player's armoury.

Finally, as we said at the outset, it can be seen as an unglamorous position, the destructive player who shields and shepherds and hustles. A **commitment** to undertaking that task is therefore very necessary.

Central Midfielder

Stamina is a must. Old school managers refer to this as a 'good engine'; it is that ability to keep moving, supporting the attack one minute, tracking a run the next and then winning a 50/50 tackle. **Self-discipline** to make those covering runs is important, as is an **eye for a goal.** Central midfielders will often be the player who arrives let into a goal scoring position and is therefore not picked up. The full gamut of **passing** skills are crucial, since plays will often gather pace as a result of a central midfielder's pass or run.

Wide Midfielder

This position has evolved from the traditional winger these days. The **speed** of a winger is required, but also a **defensive discipline** to get back into shape when possession is lost. Making **runs** during a transition to regaining possession is important, because the ball will often be switched to a wide player, as that is where the space is. **Crossing ability, shooting skills and dribbling skills and techniques** are essential factors, An **eye for a goal** is important, to take some of the pressure off of the centre forward. **Passing** is also a skill much in demand from this position.

Winger

Sometimes seen as a luxury these days, nevertheless a winger can win matches. All of the attacking qualities listed above are required, but because the job of a winger is almost exclusively attacking, extra **pace**, better **shooting** and so on is expected.

Number Ten

In the old days, this player would be known as the second striker; in the present game the number ten is the playmaker, the maestro, the glamour player – even more so than the centre forward. A number ten possesses outstanding **close control**, because the ball is often received in tight situations. Superb short and long **passing** is needed. This position is expected to produce goals as well as assists, and therefore strong **shooting** is needed, as well as the ability to make great **runs** and have an **eye for a goal**.

Reading of the game is vital, as the number ten is the player who often 'sees' the pass that opens a defence.

Still important, but perhaps not crucial to possess all, the attributes of **speed, heading, defensive discipline** when possession is lost and **tracking back** are all useful.

Centre forward

There are broadly two kinds of centre forward. The Olivier Giroud type – the French striker is a colossus who can **hold up the ball** well, **head** with excellence, score goals and also bring in other players with his **reading** of the game. Giroud is phenomenally **strong** and **brave**, giving nothing in his tussles with defenders. He is also a useful **defender** in set plays, using his physique and **defensive heading** ability to great effect.

The other kind is best characterised by Lionel Messi. The goal scoring wonder has **explosive** pace, great **dribbling** ability and superb **balance**.

On top of this, any centre forward needs **an eye for a goal**, great **shooting** ability and excellent **close** control.

Putting It Together

Once the analytics have been completed, a coach can see the picture of his squad. He or she can select their preferred formation based on the strengths of the players they have available. A lot of skilful centre backs? Play three and give them the licence to get forward. Struggling to find a quality central defensive midfielder? Choose a formation that negates the need for such a player, such as going for 4-5-1 or even 4-4-2.

But we all know that the best eleven technical players do not always make the best team. In making the final decision, the coach needs to consider the way players work together. He will consider their **communication**, their **resilience** and **fighting spirit.**

It will be these factors that are the final piece in the jigsaw of formation. Next comes the tinkering, the adapting of a formation to tackle the threats of the opposition. If they play a ball on the deck, fast passing type of game, then stamina in our own team becomes even more important because the ball will move around more quickly. If they play a high pressing game then better **first touch** and **control** is required from every player, since there will be constant pressure, rather than just in the final third as would be the case with a side that stands off.

With the information of every player's abilities, choosing that formation is more informed, more objective and therefore, in all likelihood, more effective.

Attacking Set Play Analytics

In this chapter we look at set plays from attacking perspectives. We will consider corners, free kicks in direct shooting positions, free kicks from wide angles, attacking throw ins and penalties.

Overall, more than one in three goals scored are from set plays, a very significant number, and therefore preparing for these situations is definitely worthwhile. Or is it?

Corners

We know the scene. A goal down and desperately searching for the equalizer. Our side wins a corner. The crowd go wild, the players' adrenaline flows. But it shouldn't really. Because, in fact, the chances of a goal are pretty remote. In fact, only one in two hundred goals in professional football results from a corner. That information comes from analytics in action. A reason for this low scoring rate is that nearly nine out of ten shots from corners (which includes headers) miss the target. That is a far higher percentage than in open play.

But the reason is quite logical if one considers it. Teams defend corners with numbers, so getting the ball through a crowd of players is tricky enough on its own, but the team attacking are also under pressure. The ball comes to the attacker with defenders close in attendance. There is little time to get into position, let alone get the ball under control.

Analytical data shows that the best corner, statistically, is the short corner. This is because defences will send out a second player to deal with these. The consequence is that there are two less players struggling to compete in the box – one from each side. That leaves more space and so increases the likelihood of any shot or header being accurate. If a long corner is to be taken, then an in swinger (a cross that starts on a curve away from goal, then swings back towards it) is more likely to result in a goal than an out swinger. This data runs against the traditional view that an out swinger is a better option because it makes it harder for the keeper to claim the ball.

However, there is not yet sufficient data to know whether the in swinger is more dangerous because defences are expecting the ball to swing outwards and so are less prepared.

The implications for the coach, or individual player, is to carry out their own analytics on their team to see which players are the most accurate in swingers of the ball. The second task is to see which set of movements lead to the box becoming least crowded, increasing the chances for a clean header or shot for the attacking side.

Direct Shot Free Kicks

If over a third of goals result from set plays, then the majority of those goals are a result of a direct free kicks. A higher percentage of penalties are converted, but there are far fewer of these compared to direct free kicks in shooting positions.

We can use analytics to both identify the best position for a kick and the best type of kick to perform. We can then use the study of our own players to identify who is the best person to take the kicks, depending on where they are.

Starting with the analysis of the kick itself, the most successful are those struck with a 'curve' kick. Our analytics are therefore looking to identify our players who can best perform this technique. Players themselves can work on this. A curve kick is created with a wide run up, the non-kicking foot planted firmly on the angle of the run and the ball struck with a firm strike across the face, imparting spin. The leg should continue through the action and end in a high position. This way, both side spin and top spin are applied, and the ball is most likely to avoid the wall while either moving away from the keeper or finding the corner of the goal.

But analytical studies further give us details of where the best free kicks entered the goal. The most successful area is the top corner, perhaps that is unsurprising. Low down in the corner was second. Few free kicks are scored, at elite level at least, unless the shot is in the corner, and mid-height is the easiest area for a keeper to make a save.

The faster the velocity of the ball the more likely it is to end in a goal. Instep shots are more accurate, but is it found that the velocity they impart is much less than with a curve free kick, and so goalkeepers can more easily save them, even though they are more likely to be on target.

Therefore, our player analytics are seeking a player who can perform the kick, generate power and provide accuracy. Simple! Most goals come from free kicks in line with the D of the penalty area. Where wider kicks are still taken with a shot, most goals came at the near post. Far post goals from wide areas were most often scored with a shot/cross that bounces in front of the keeper. Because of the trajectory of this kind of delivery keepers leave it late to dive, in case a striker or defender gets a touch goalwards on the ball.

It was found that the optimum distance from goal for a shot to be converted is 27 metres. A high percentage of goals from free kicks which are taken as shots come from deflections. Less than might be expected are from rebounds, perhaps because shots are often high and where a keeper makes a save, it is likely to go out for a corner.

Nearly all goals scored from a shot directly taken at the free kick entered the goal within a meter of the post.

Now we know what to tell our free kick takers to do. And we can assess, using our analytics, the best players to deliver those requirements.

Wide Angle Free Kicks

When John Henry took over the running of Liverpool Football Club, one of the most famous and successful of all time, but one that had slipped from the highest echelons of the sport, he thought that the use of analytics could drive the team back to the head of the world game. As owner of the Boston Red Sox team, he had employed a system called 'Moneyball' to deliver good results in the world of Baseball. This system identified the most effective play and sought to use it as often as practicable.

Using statistical data, he identified the two best crossers of the ball in the game, and the best converter of crosses, and spent a lot of money buying them. These were Jordan Henderson, Stewart Downing and, in the middle, Andy Carroll. All were internationals, but none would merit the accolade of being 'world class'. The experiment failed miserably; yes, they did their jobs well, but the job they were doing was, in footballing terms, not very effective. Crosses are not a productive way of increasing the flow of goals. Henry had learned that there were far more variables in the more fluid game of soccer.

Statistically, this raises the question of wide area free kicks. These are most dangerous where they are in line with the edge of the penalty area and the attacking team possesses both strong and effective headers of the ball, and players who can deliver fast, in swinging crosses. The closer to the corner flag the free kick is, the more like a corner it becomes – and we know that these are not effective. The deeper it is, the longer the ball takes to get into the box and so the more time defences have to get in position to deal with it, and the more time the keeper has to come and collect or clear the ball.

Using analytics derived from analysis of many, many matches we can see therefore that the only time to hit the free kick directly into the box is if we have both (a) the kinds of players to deliver a good ball, and others able to get on the end of the cross, and (b) when the ball is in a narrow field of between around twelves and twenty-five yards from the by line. Other wide free kicks, statistically, are more effective played short and fast, utilizing the fact that a defence will be trying to get organized, and therefore not necessarily expecting a quick pass.

Throw Ins

Attacking throw ins can lead to goal scoring possibilities because they can be rehearsed. Our own analysis of our players can determine whether the long throw is likely to be a significant weapon. Note, there are three factors which need to be performed by the thrower to make this kind of weapon effective. Firstly, the player must be able to throw the ball with considerable accuracy. The ball needs to enter the area the team has rehearsed to ensure that the right player is there to meet it, and the runs off the ball by the second and third receivers end up with the flicked-on throw reaching them.

Secondly, the throw needs to be long. It needs to arrive in a position where the recipient can flick the ball into a goal scoring area. Finally, the thrower needs to be able to generate speed. A flat, fast throw is far harder to defend against than a loopy long throw.

The next consideration to make is whether the team has players tall enough and strong enough in the air to win that throw. Finally, the opposition needs to be considered. If they have a keeper who is strong at coming out and clearing long throws, then they will be less effective that with a keeper who prefers to stay on their line. Equally, a big defensive set up with lots of players who are good in the air will see less positive results than against a smaller (even if more mobile) set up.

However, throw ins do not just have to be long to create a goal scoring chance. The other type of attacking throw, analytics demonstrate, that can cause problems to a defence is the quick throw. This is because the defending team is less organized, and if the ball can be back in play before that organization is restored, then there will be more spaces into which attackers can run.

Penalties

Of all set plays, the penalty is the easiest to analyze, because there are the fewest number of variables. But there is an interesting twist to this aspect of the game. It is the only point in a game where the striker is expected to score, and the maneuver is planned and happens with time for the striker to think. With free kicks, the expectation is that the striker will not score, it is a bonus when he does. In normal play, there are more variables and less time to think so instinct (that 'eye for a goal') becomes of greater importance.

Therefore, with a penalty, it is not just the best striker of a ball who should become the nominated taker, but one who is calm, or even more effective, striking under pressure. While we know that practice makes some difference to a player's ability to score penalties, the pressure of a match cannot be replicated in a training situation.

Therefore, the coach could use his or her analytical data to try to determine the player who is most adept at striking the ball combined with a cool head. Yet penalties are even more complicated than that. To be awarded a spot kick when already 3-0 up puts far less pressure on the taker than when the scores are level, or the team is a goal behind.

The penalty shoot out provides a wholly different level of pressure, and although they happen rarely in the entire gamut of matches played, coaches need to use their data on 'coolness under pressure' and 'clean striking of the ball' to help them determine the order of players to take their spot kick.

The best player should not be saved until last. Firstly, there is the risk that the shoot-out could be decided prior to that, and therefore the team's best taker misses out on a chance to score. Secondly, the pressure ratchets up to maximum level from usually the third kick, because this is the point at which scoring becomes essential to keep a side in the game.

Depending on the level at which a team plays, and the resources available to it, two further sets of data can be used to maximize the chances of converting a penalty kick into a goal.

Firstly, is data from one's own side. Assuming the psychological factors have already been assessed, it is easy enough to measure the accuracy, power and scoring percentages of players in a team. That can be done with pen and paper. On top of that, the data of where a penalty taker prefers to place the ball can also be used.

Where clubs have access to such details, the opposition's strengths and preferences can be taken into account. Particularly where the opposition goalkeeper likes to dive. Thus, if two players on our team have reasonably even sets of data, but one player prefers putting the ball to a keeper's left, but that is where that particular keeper favors his dive, then it makes sense to promote the other member of our team, the one who likes hitting it to the right, to penalty taker for that match. Players themselves can also use the data, working on hitting their penalties to the side not favored by the keeper they are facing.

It is these tiny percentage factors that can combine to produce a winning formula using data.

Defending penalties can also be improved through study by goalkeepers. If they know where strikers prefer to hit their shots, they increase their chance of saving them. Statistically, it is also a reasonable idea for a goalkeeper to sometimes remain upright for a penalty. More are hit straight down the middle than is often given credit for, and once the keeper dives, he is beaten.

There was very clear evidence of the use of data in a positive way by a keeper in the 2012 Champions' League Cup Final. Chelsea were victorious over Bayern Munich in a shoot-out. Their outstanding goalkeeper had spent many hours studying a video of five years of Bayern Munich penalties (a fine piece of data gathering by somebody!). He knew the favored strike angle of every player in their team who took a penalty. He used this data to guess where the penalties would be placed. He guessed the angle correctly every time, suggesting that the word 'guessed' is a little disparaging to the science that had gone into his own preparation. In going the right way, he saved two of the penalties, enough to win the shoot-out.

Having looked at the important role of set plays from an attacking perspective, we will now look at what analytics can tell us about defending these aspects of the game.

Defensive Set Play Analytics

In looking at defending set plays, we will focus on the same aspects as in the chapter just read. However, we included a look at penalties from the goalkeeper's viewpoint and so that element is already covered.

Shots From Direct Free Kicks

The fact is, that if the shot is good enough, there is nothing that can be done to prevent the goal. However, we can use analytics to reduce the chance of a score by doing all we can to stop the imperfect attempt.

Don't Concede The Free Kick In the First Place

When selecting our defence and defensive midfield, this is a factor we can consider. Since a high percentage of goals come from set plays, we can choose players who statistically give away fewer free kicks in dangerous positions. We are looking for defensive players with good self-discipline, who are not going to dive into tackles unless it is absolutely necessary. Pep Guardiola, former Barcelona manager and one of the world's most successful team leaders, rarely advocates tackling at all, more harrying for the ball, and putting on pressure to make the opposition lose the ball. The only time he would advocate a full-on tackle is when it is to prevent a goal scoring opportunity. We are looking for players with good balance and agility, and fair pace, so that it is less likely that they can be drawn into committing a foul.

Organize The Wall

Walls do a good job in preventing the ball reaching the target. Ideally, tall players should be in the wall to prevent them having to jump (thus leaving the risk of the shot underneath the wall).

Stay Alert For Rebounds

A couple of players should be allocated the role of making sure that they are first to rebounds. These cannot be too deep or attacking players will be able to legitimately block the keeper's view.

Wide Angle Free Kicks And Corners

There are two main schools of thought with regards to defending corners and set play balls into the box from wide positions. The first advocates man marking. The second is zonal marking.

Man Marking

This works on the basis of each defender taking responsibility for an attacker. It is a risky ploy because attackers can combine prior to the ball being struck to protect the 'target' player from marking. It has the advantage of meaning that the defender is moving and can therefore jump higher than were he taking a standing start.

Zonal Marking

Under this system, each defender is responsible for an area of the penalty box and seeks to ensure that if the ball is reachable in their zone, then they will get their heads on it. The main problem with this system is that the defenders are starting from a stationary position, whereas the attacker has a run on the ball, therefore getting height into the jump is harder.

Those who enjoy watching elite football on television and then listening to the pundits at their end will frequently hear criticism of the zonal marking system. This is perhaps because when it is successful, it is less dramatic than a man marked clearance. The ball simply fails to reach its target. Perhaps also, when goals are scored against a zonal defence, the defender may appear weak because the striker has simply got above them.

The statistics, revealed by the analytics, tell a different story. Zonal marking is more successful. The difference is marginal, but it is there.

The Best Approach

If they are using the evidence of analytics, teams should employ a zonal defence. However, the evidence also shows the risks of the system, as described above. Therefore, particular targets for the attack should also be man marked. It does not have to be the best header of a ball but should be somebody mobile and strong. The presence of such a player should limit the leap of the striker, thus allowing the zonal defence to do its job.

Other Positions To Secure

One of the big debates is whether or not to put a defender on the line. Statistics suggest that this is advisable on the far post; the near post should only be covered if the ball is hit beyond this position, when a defender should drop back onto the post until the ball is cleared.

It is important to place a player outside the near post to cut off the near post corner, or the low driven cross, or even the mis hit corner. This player is often the one who makes the clearance.

The same applies with the delivery of a wide free kick.

Throw Ins

Long Throws

This is a situation where in play analytics come to the fore. It is likely that the attacking team will have a set play. They are relying on their target man winning the ball, then scoring off the second ball. The target man is therefore likely to make the same run each time.

The coach and defenders need to learn the move that the opponents are making and ensure that their best header of the ball is the one who challenges the target man, and players are there to pick up and clear the second ball.

Analytics will tell us that a throw is more accurate than a kick. Therefore, where there is a player on the opposition side who can deliver a fast, flat throw, it is something very hard to defend against. The player on the defence with the biggest advantage is the goalkeeper, as this is the player who can get the extra height from using hands. Therefore, the goalkeeper should be the player to come for the ball and look to clear unless this draws him or her too far from their goal.

Quick Throws

Other then training a team to get organized quickly, there is little to do to defend this. Encouraging decision making is the best way, so players are prepared to slot into gaps, even if it is not their position, to neutralize the threat of a quick throw.

Player Performance Analytics

We can build up profiles of our players very effectively. This data can then be put into software programmes – the market is growing – which will analyse the results and show graphically individual, group and team strengths and weaknesses. This data can be used, if the circumstances allow, to inform tactical play, the best ways to counter opponents' strengths: where clubs operate in this way, it can help with recruitment policy.

However, for small club sides, or individual players in small clubs, the data can be analysed without recourse to specialist software. Conclusions from data may be less accurate, and mistakes are more likely to be made, but the information found will still be useful for players and coaches to identify the strengths, weaknesses and contribution to the team a player can make.

We should look at performance both in matches and training, and that data can be used to analyse the relationship between to two for a player. It will also demonstrate the roles pressure and competition play in influencing a team member's performance.

In the match situation, assessing data where complex tracking equipment is not available is still possible. A good way can be to allocate a club operative, injured player, assistant coach – even a reliable supporter – to follow the performance of his or her player, looking out for and recording the criteria to be assessed.

Questions For Consideration When Collecting Player Data

It is important to be as objective as possible when collecting data. These are the kinds of question that should be considered when taking, and analysing, that information. We have referred to human observed data below as 'expert' data, since the person taking the information is using their expertise to make judgements.

- How comparable and reliable is expert data compared to electronically generated data?
- How are experts making their judgements?
- What attributes of a player seem to be most influential in their performance.
- Do different positions on the park require different attributes, and if so, what are they?
- Does combining individual rating enable a team rating to be achieved?
- Do the experts consider the outcome of the game when evaluating individual performances?

Once these questions have been answered, the conclusions can be added to the evaluations carried out, making them a more accurate indicator of a player's ability.

What Do We Look For When Assessing A Player?

This is an important question, and the answer is straightforward. A lot! It is important to get a rounded picture of the player, and therefore all of the following could be considered as important. However, coaches may choose to concentrate on certain aspects of a player's performance and ability (as might the player themselves) to develop this, or because that is something that needs addressing in the team or because positionally it is most important.

The full range of considerations are below:

Basic Characteristics

These are the non-soccer specific factors which may play a part in a player's performance.

- Nationality/language for communication
- Age
- Height

- Stronger foot
- Playing positions

Attacking Skills

- Ball control
- Dribbling control
- Dribbling speed
- Low/Ground level pass
- Lofted Passing
- Attacking headers
- Turning speed
- Turning Skills (this could be sub divided to include different types of turn such as a Cruyff turn)
- Dribbling skills (for example, a scissors, nutmeg or feint)
- Close range finishing
- Penalty area shooting
- Long distance shooting
- Ability to impart swerve on the ball
- Shooting with weaker foot accuracy
- Shooting with weaker foot power
- Shooting with weaker foot confidence
- Dead ball shooting
- Dead ball delivery

- Explosive power
- Acceleration
- Speed
- Quality of runs
- Willingness to run off the ball
- Ability to cross early
- Ability to pass early
- One touch passing
- First time shooting (this can be sub divided into the shooting categories above)

Defensive Characteristics

- Positioning
- Reading and anticipation
- Defensive prowess
- Ball winning
- Kick power
- Heading distance
- Jump
- Heading under pressure
- Strength
- Man Marking

Goalkeeping

- Handling
- Punching
- Anticipation
- Reactions
- Communication
- Speed
- Recovery from dive
- Strength diving each side
- Bravery
- Kicking distance
- Kicking accuracy
- Kicking confidence
- Throwing distance
- Throwing accuracy

General Characteristics (soccer)

- Form
- How prone to injury?
- Recovery from injury
- Long throw
- Ability to track back

- Balance
- Stamina
- Weighted passing

General Characteristics (nonspecific)

- Fighting spirit
- Resilience
- Disciplinary control
- Captaincy strengths
- Impact as a substitute
- Communication

Clearly, a coach may wish to weight these characteristics depending on the needs of his team and the way he wishes to play. A good example occurred with the manager Pep Guardiola. The former Barcelona and Bayern Munich manager, widely regarded to be the world's best currently, took over the immensely wealthy club Manchester City. His goalkeeper was the well-regarded England international 'keeper Joe Hart. However, he decided that he needed another man between the posts. The crucial factor was that Guardiola likes to play a possession-based game with play starting from the back. He also likes to push his defenders forwards. Therefore, he needed a footballing goalkeeper. One who could receive a pass back with confidence, could pass well himself, could even beat an on-rushing attacker. It was vital to Guardiola's playing plan that the ball was never booted forward in hope rather than specific intent.

Unfortunately for Hart, although he is a fine goalkeeper with excellent handling and shot stopping skills, his football skills are middling at best.

Equally, at any level, a coach might decide that his team needs a big centre half capable of dominating at set plays. He may be prepared to sacrifice another attribute to get this, such as speed or passing ability. Where his team already has height, he will want other skills from this position.

We can see that it is very clear that such a detailed analysis of a player's abilities will lead to a clear plan for his or her own improvement. It will also show clearly what the player can offer to the team. By combining the data of the entire team, overall strengths and weaknesses can be better detected. Software will do this quickly and effectively. Many of the programmes are now affordable, and sufficiently straightforward to be used by those in the amateur game, even in the lower echelons of the sport.

Indeed, those who undertake analytics, apply the findings intelligently and invest the time (plus, perhaps, money) needed to gain effective results may well find themselves leaving the lower echelons behind.

Player Injury Analytics

The four biggest leagues in the soccer world are all in Europe. The English Premier League is the strongest, at least when it comes to money; La Liga tends to return the best teams, although that is down to Barcelona and Real Madrid. The Bundesliga in Germany is very strong, as is Serie A, the Italian league that pulsates success with periods of dominance and spells when it is much less strong. In the 2015 season the cost of injuries in each of those leagues averaged nearly $70 million.

Better pitches and more understanding of training regimes and external factors such as diet and psychology have seen injury situations improve, but the increased competitiveness, number of matches and speed of players has countered this.

Into the world of player injuries now comes big data from analytics – and it is making a difference. Across the sporting world, we are seeing a reduction in injury rates of up to a third, with soft tissue type injuries falling by close to 90%.

The systems are still in their infancy, and sports scientists are still learning how best to interpret data. However, the basic idea is that by collecting extensive data, large software companies are able to identify the patterns which lead to injury. All clubs can make use of that data to best protect their own players.

Durability

Injuries occur most when players become physically and mentally tired. Muscles are more like to strain, or tear, when players reach the end of their stamina. This has two implications for the player and coach. Firstly, they need to develop their stamina through a fitness programme that means they can last for ninety minutes. At professional level, this is relatively easy since trackers can be applied in training to identify the point at which a player is tiring. At an amateur level, there is more instinct involved, but benefits will still be gained.

Mental exhaustion is also a contributor to injury, in two ways. Firstly, when mentally tired judgement suffers, and players can over stretch or mis time tackles. Secondly, a fit player is more likely to be injured by a tired opponent. This is best avoided by ensuring that players can mentally stay focussed throughout the game, helping them to avoid the mis timed tackle or lunge.

Technique

Good technique is crucial. Without this, players run a greater risk of pulling muscles or causing strains. But even more than this, poor technique can lead to long term wear and tear injuries, some of which can be career threatening. A good case in point can be applied to the former striker Michael Owen. The England, Liverpool, Real Madrid, Newcastle and Manchester United striker promised to turn into perhaps the best in the world.

His game was built around explosive pace, but this was lost after an injury. He remained a fine player, but that edge was gone from his game. Eventually, the problem was traced to poor posture which has placed long term strain on muscles, from which he never fully recovered.

Poor technique also leads a player to expose themselves more to injury in the tackle. Analytics can really help here. The player's technique in various skills can be analysed, and where there are faults, these can be addressed with practice.

Flexibility

The role of stretching is much better known now. Effective stretching can be added to training routines and adapted to the particular needs of individual players and positions, identified through the analysis of their attributes and the demands of the position.

Predictive Injury Prevention

Sometimes, when teams are announced, fans can be very frustrated. Their best player is left out or, even more frustratingly, left on the bench. 'Why?' they wonder 'If he's fit enough for the bench, he's fit enough to play.'

High level analytics, as are gained through tracking devices used in training, can in fact identify that a player may only be fit enough for half a game, so he is saved in case he is needed. The analytics may have identified an increased risk of long term injury following a minor knock or strain.

No team likes to be without its best players, and no player likes to sit out six matches because they took a risk on a dodgy knee or minor hamstring problem. Therefore, the use of analytics can help to prevent injury in the first place and help to stop it returning when a recovery appears to be in place.

It provides a detailed analysis for the individual regarding fitness, technique and flexibility. In addition, empirical (big data) evidence can be applied in a more general sense to understand likely full recovery times.

Player Combination Analytics

Barcelona do not win every match, even ones that are not against Real Madrid. The team at the bottom of the English Premier League sometimes beat the league leaders. There are shocks in cups when lower league teams beat their more talented top division opponents. A couple of years ago, Leicester City won the Premier league with a team that had only just escaped relegation the year before.

How? The answer is, as we know, that soccer is a team game, and the team is stronger than eleven individuals.

Therefore, player combinations can add significantly to a team's success. We can use soccer analytics to identify the best player combinations from the talent at our disposal.

Which Data Matters?

This is very important. Data is of little use if it just describes what has happened. It only becomes useful when it identifies the causes of decisive actions on the pitch.

As old school pundits are keen on telling us, there is only one statistic that matters – goals scored against goals conceded.

In some ways they are right, in others their view is too simplistic. We need to go back to see what leads to those goals, and the answer is usually team play. Similarly, if we look at what prevents those chances from happening, it is usually team play. Certainly, there are occasions when a player will pick up the ball from the half way line, beat three players and bury the ball in the bottom corner. Or, will hit a 30-yard volley into the roof of the net direct from a headed clearance. On rare occasions a goalkeeper will make a simply unbelievable reaction save. But mostly, it is about teamwork.

It is passes and dribbles that lead to the goal scoring opportunities, it is solid defending and covering that stops those chances from occurring.

That means getting the combination of players right is very important. We need to look at passing accuracy, dribbling skills and how runs off the ball supports these. We need to look at players who pass to each other regularly, reading each other's plans. Defensively, we need to look again at pairs and blocks of players that cover well for each other. A part of that will be communication. We should analyse the spaces between midfielders, midfielders and defenders, and between defenders themselves. These are the factors which will lead to goal scoring opportunities, and conversely stop them from occurring.

How To Judge Player Combinations

There is some theory involved here, and also use of the data gathered from team mates playing together, both in practice and in matches. The theory element requires us to consider the best distances between players for optimal defensive capability; and when attacking, the best positions to get into to make a decisive pass that creates a goal scoring opportunity.

Mesut Ozil has topped the number of chance creating passes for most of the last six or seven seasons across all of Europe's top leagues. It is not therefore surprising that he has just secured a pay structure breaking pay rise from his current club, Arsenal.

From analysing the data, we collect from different groups of players working together we can assess, statistically at least, the best combinations for our team. However, there is also a psychological factor in choosing player combinations. A team does not have to be made up of best mates, but there does need to be trust between team mates. A part of that comes from quality; we are more likely to pass to a player who is going to do something with that pass. Another element comes from work rate – we are going to be more comfortable sharing defensive midfield with a partner who works hard to cover runs, make tackles, shepherds and harasses than with one who leaves the bulk of the work to ourselves, however good they are on the ball. And finally, there is the undefinable element, the way that certain players naturally understand what their partners will do. That skill improves with playing together, and from training together.

The message to the coach here is that once partnerships are established, it is a good idea to stick with them.

The Use Of Substitutions To Change A Game

We can employ substitutes to replace tired and injured players, or to make a tactical change to protect a lead or recover a deficit. There has been a good deal of research into this area, and we now know the times to make statistically the most impact.

Bearing in mind that there is a less than even chance that the game will change as the result of a substitution, if it is going to then statistics suggest the first one cannot be later than the 58th minute. The second needs to follow by the 73rd minute mark – it can be earlier, but not later. Then the final substitution happens in the 79th minute or before.

Case Studies

In this chapter we will look at some examples of analytics used at the professional level.

Case Study One – Using Statistical Analysis to Promote Increased Success With Particular Moves – Challenging Pre Conceptions

Two short examples here of how simple analysis, the sort that any keen soccer fan can carry out, can demonstrate the difference between instinct and reality.

Corners: Not many goals come from corners. But when Manchester City, full of the Middle Eastern dollars of their benevolent owner, were scoring none their analysts tried to find out why.

At the time, Manchester City were mostly working on outswinging corners. When these work, the headed goal that follows is impressive. A pure strike, the keeper left in no man's land, the clean contact sending the header into the net. Unfortunately, that doesn't happen often, although when it does, it sticks in the mind.

The analysts studied thousands of videos of corners – the sort of thing any coach can do on cable TV, or via video clips. Their discovery was that inswinging corners where around three to four times more successful. Yes, the goals scored were often own goals, the ball deflecting off a defender, or keeper errors made under pressure. Usually, these goals were scrappy. They did not stick in the mind of coaches. But the truth for a top professional team is no different than for the Sunday league side full of sales people, teachers and mechanics. The ball hit to the near post – right footer from the left, and vice versa – will result in more goals than the opposite delivery.

Unfortunately for Manchester City's fans and players. Manuel Pellegrini, coach at the time, was not easily persuaded. The team's approach to corners remained unchanged, the very occasional good goal being used to support the system. Pellegrini left the club, replaced, not too much later. Perhaps the two events were partly connected.

Penalty shoot outs are often the differences between progression to the later stages of competitions and going home. There have been numerous studies examining the best way take penalties – visualisation, practice and so forth, but analytics can add an extra dimension. Studies reported on the website ucanalytics.com demonstrate that, in the decisive penalty of a shoot out, goalkeepers remain at the centre of their goal just 2% of the time (as opposed to moving to their left on 57% of occasions, and 41% to their right); this is almost certainly because the pressure to make the key save pushes them one way or another. They chose positive action rather than hoping for a straight shot. Interestingly, the decisive penalty in a shoot out has only a 44% success rate, much lower than the average of 75%. Thus, by employing these analytics we can advise our decisive taker to hit the ball straight – he should then score 98% of the time!

Until, of course, goalkeepers discover that this is the double bluff their opponents will use.

Case Study Two – Charles Hughes: When Analytics Fail to Tell the Truth

It goes without saying that the bigger the sample used in studying soccer analytics, the more often the truth will be revealed. Smaller samples can be used to form hypothesis, and to promote ideas for further testing, but in the case of Charles Hughes, technical director of football at the English Football Association, a failure to use a satisfactory sample led to the stultification of the English game, and the negation of possibly the strongest generation of footballers to ever don the three lions shirt.

Hughes was always an advocate of the long ball game. Certainly, back in the 1970s and before, the astonishingly bad quality of pitches in Britain contributed to this. While European and South American players were developing high quality skills in control, passing and shooting on firm, flat surfaces, the waterlogged mud that constituted the typical British grass roots playing field gave little opportunity for the development of such skills. Simply, the bounce of the ball was unpredictable, the carry of the ball virtually impossible to judge.

The result had been, for generations, easy to predict. Taken back to school boy level, those who progressed best were not necessarily the ones with the most potential or even actual talent. They were the boys who were big, strong, athletic; who could kick a ball a long distance and chase it down more quickly than their peers. By the time puberty came and went, and physical strength became more of a level playing field (which was, as we have seen, a rather unusual occurrence in 1950s Britain) the small, skilful players were often lost to the game. Of course, some progressed to the highest professional level. George Best, Alan Ball and Bobby Moore are three famous examples. But the pool from which to pick was smaller, and therefore the strength of the British game lacked depth.

The result of all this was that British teams were typically filled with big, strong men who were powerful athletes but not always the smartest players. Consequentially, there was no drive to produce carpets for these men (there were not many women playing, in those days) to show case their talents. So even at professional level, pitches often resembled a farmer's field after harvest than a pool table. Witness Ronnie Radford's goal, in the early 1970s, for Hereford United against Newcastle, in what was at the time the major soccer tournament in the country, the FA cup. (https://www.youtube.com/watch?v=ZnjEmscMDR4) Certainly, we can admire the goal, but note the pitch from which it was struck. How could such conditions be allowed to flourish?

Of course, elsewhere in the world, they were not. So when it came to the biggest stages – European club competition, world cups and European championships, England, the birthplace of soccer – became inconsequential.

Ironically, it was one of the very acts of sporting vandalism carried out by Britain's first female Prime Minister, Margaret Thatcher, that led to change. Thatcher was not a fan of soccer, nor those from the lower echelons of society. The one escape from classroom failure the kids of the 1970s and early 1980s had was the twice weekly games session. But if Thatcher did not hugely like sport, she did approve of making money. As a result, local authorities throughout the land sold their school playing fields to developers. Soon the only goals left were being sold from the retail warehouses that flew up, or appeared in miniature form in the gardens of the 'executive' houses that were now cramped onto the nearby school's once outdoor space.

Something had to be done. Clubs got involved, along with enterprise – social and business – and proper artificial pitches began to appear; those grass areas left had to cope with even greater demand than before – the only way for this to happen was for them to be properly looked after.

Matters for English soccer began to look up. The 'golden generation' of Paul Scholes, the Neville Brothers, David Beckham, Gary Linekar, Paul Gascoigne and, later, Rio Ferdinand, Frank Lampard and Steven Gerrard was on the horizon.

Then, in the early 1990s, Charles Hughes came to prominence, and English soccer was cast back two decades. The context to our case study is important, because only by understanding this can the true dangers of poor interpretation of analytics be properly understood.

Hughes was deeply influenced by the thoughts of a man with little connection to soccer. Charles Reep was a WW2 wing commander with an interest in the game who is considered by most as the father of the long ball. With not much evidence, he deduced that most goals resulted from three or less passes, and so advocated getting the ball forward as quickly as possible.

Hughes' conclusions were based on analysis of only around 100 matches, far too few upon which to base a national system of play. He picked the games from various sources, including the Brazil team. From his small source he identified two themes:

- Most goals come from five or fewer passes
- Most goals are scored from the 'Position of Maximum Opportunity, which he called POMO

From this, he deduced (and wrote many books on the subject) that the secret to success was to get the ball to the POMO as quickly as possible, as from there goals would inevitably flow. Unfortunately, Hughes' approach is now considered (rightly) flawed. He used an insufficient sample; he applied data that supported his theories; he overlooked other factors, such as pitch and weather conditions, the technical skills and pace of players, the ease with which coaches could tactically nullify the POMO. As a result, English players of a generation were required to simply pump the ball into a POMO (largely, a zone behind the defence) as quickly as possible, Fine skills and technique were once more neglected – this time as a result of policy rather than necessity – and English soccer lingered longer in the doldrums

Despite the national team's repeated failure, his influence was such that even national coaches, all of whom had more experience of soccer than he, found their official support evapiorating if they wandered from Hughes' prescriptive approach.

Case Study Three – Pure Analytics

Our final case study uses an example which might be beyond the remit of many amatueur and youth teams. Nevertheless, it illustrates the value added benefit effective use of analytics can bring to a team.

Derry is a small city in Northern Ireland. It's soccer team is the only one to compete in the Irish Premier league. The club is professional but draws many of its players from its locality; it really should not be able to compete against the likes of teams from bigger cities of Cork and Dublin, but it does, maintaining a position in the league. This is thanks, in large part, to the 'moneyball' effect provided through effective use of analytics.

During the time of the case study, which is recent, Derry employed a data analyist to support the team. In particular, it made use of a professional analytics system called PerformaSports which enabled extensive video analysis of match, team and individual player performance.

As both the coach of the team, Kenny Shiels, and a number of players, stated, during the intensity of match play, specifics of performance can be missed. Also, it is the nature of people to interpret on-going action from their own, often biased, viewpoint. Thus, it would be normal to view a loss of possession as coming from an unpunished piece of foul play by the opposition. However, video analysis provides objective evidence. So, for example, it could be that a player is receiving the ball with their body in the wrong position, and thus finding it hard to retain possession.

The data analysis is used by Derry City in five specific ways:

- To analyse individual performance, highlighting strengths and weaknesses of a player. This evidence is then used by players and coaches to develop bespoke drills and work outs to address the weaknesses, while the strengths are integrated more often into team play. Thus, it might become apparent that a striker needs to work on acceleration over the first five metres when given through balls. Speed work can then be prioritised. Equally, it may become apparent that a wing back delivers crosses with a high degree of accuracy. Team play can then be developed to maximise the opportunities for crosses from this player.
- To analyse performance by units in the team. For example, video analysis might demonstrate that the defence struggles to move up as a unit, leaving opponents both onside, and in space. Communication drills can then be applied to improve this area.

- Team play. Through whole team analysis, evidence can be seen of, for example, the effectiveness of the high press Derry sought to use. Where opponents were able to play out of the high press, the reason is identified and appropriate drills put in place to address this.
- To identify strengths of opponents. Video clips were used of both individual and team play. For example, the Derry right back explained how he studied clips of his opposing winger, to identify their favoured foot, their preference for dribbling or passing early. Coach Shiels explained how video footage of opponents is used to inform specific coaching in the interval between matches.
- To identify opportunities for creating chances. Again, the footage was used effectively to identify weaknesses in opponents. For example, in one case it was seen that the centre halves pressed high, but lacked pace on the turn. This encouraged Derry to create chances by putting the ball in the space behind them, for strikers and midfielders to run on to.

The use of the analytics for Derry followed a fairly prescribed method. Firstly, clips of individual performances were distributed so that players could identify their own strengths and weaknesses, and work on their own individual training programmes. Next, whole squad sessions focussed on team performance, making use of earlier matches as well when common strengths or weaknesses were identified. Training was then tinkered with to exploit the information they had. Next, footage of opponents was analysed with the squad, and training adapted once again with the next match specifically in mind. Typically, the squad would hold three full video analysis sessions per week, plus individual sessions.

Unsurprisingly, as we saw at the beginning of this case study, the use of analytics worked, enabling Derry to perform at a higher level than some bigger, richer clubs.

Conclusion

We hope that you have enjoyed this book and gained some valuable knowledge about the value of soccer analytics can offer to a team and to an individual player.

We can use analytics at any level. From a pen and paper analysis, recording what we can, to the sort of systems used at the highest levels of the professional game, where cameras track every player during a match, where trackers follow every move in training, and teams of highly paid analysts report back from their findings.

Of course, analytics in themselves are not too useful. We might see that a player can run twelve kilometres in a match; but that is only useful when we apply that information to improve the player and the team. In fact, when the data is turned into metrics, that is using analytics to raise quality and standards, then it becomes of considerable help to a team and its individual players.

There is a degree of resistance to the use of analytics in soccer. For many years, it fell behind other sports such as baseball, cricket and rugby. Partly, this is the fluid nature of the game – those other sports contain far more set plays and breaks in action. But also, was the feeling that soccer is a gut instinct game, a game of innovation and magic moments rather than something that can be pre-planned.

However, over time, it has been understood that analytics help to improve performance, help to improve recruitment, helps players to develop skills and reduce their chances of getting injured. That indefinable spark must still be there, or the benefits of attacking metrics will easily be countered by defensive organisation and the game will become a stale, barren sport, devoid of excitement. It happened to some extent in Rugby Union twenty-five years ago, when early data collection demonstrated the importance of territory. The game became a boring series of exchanged kicks, end to end but with no thrills. Soccer, though, has too many variables to allow that to spoil the game.

That's the great thing (one of them) about the sport. If we had a perfectly scientific match, with every side performing as the analytics suggest, then we would lose the spontaneity, the individual genius of the best players in a team. But even the million or more analytics Opta cameras take in a typical top level league match cannot tell us everything.

So, let us keep the maverick, the genius, the player who lifts the crowds to their feet. But, at any level, we can enhance other elements of the sport through applying the data we now know can shape the game.

Printed in Great Britain
by Amazon